SECRETS OF PASSING THE
NEBOSH EXAM

SECRETS OF PASSING THE
NEBOSH EXAM

Don't Study Hard, Just Study Smart.

Helbert R. Cual

PARTRIDGE

Copyright © 2018 by Helbert R. Cual.

ISBN: Hardcover   978-1-5437-4023-3
       Softcover   978-1-5437-4024-0
       eBook   978-1-5437-4025-7

All rights reserved. No part of this book may be used or reproduced by any means, graphic, electronic, or mechanical, including photocopying, recording, taping or by any information storage retrieval system without the written permission of the author except in the case of brief quotations embodied in critical articles and reviews.

Because of the dynamic nature of the Internet, any web addresses or links contained in this book may have changed since publication and may no longer be valid. The views expressed in this work are solely those of the author and do not necessarily reflect the views of the publisher, and the publisher hereby disclaims any responsibility for them.

Print information available on the last page.

To order additional copies of this book, contact
Toll Free 800 101 2657 (Singapore)
Toll Free 1 800 81 7340 (Malaysia)
orders.singapore@partridgepublishing.com

www.partridgepublishing.com/singapore

CONTENTS

Dedication vii

Acknowledgments ix

Introduction xi

How To Use This Book xv

Chapter 1   NEBOSH At A Glance 1

Chapter 2   Getting Started 17

Chapter 3   Why Do Candidates Fail In
            NEBOSH Examinations? 29

Chapter 4   Study And Preparation 33

Chapter 5   Common Pitfalls 41

Chapter 6   Overcoming Pitfalls 49

Chapter 7   Exam Techniques 55

Chapter 8   One Not-So-Common 'Freebie' 89

About The Author 93

DEDICATION

This book is dedicated to YOU!

Yes it's YOU my fellow NEBOSH candidates whose main objective is to pass the exams - **on the first take**.

Just like you, I have travelled this NEBOSH journey and by God's grace I passed it all on my first take. So in this book I'm sharing to you how I did it – and may this served as a guide in making your NEBOSH journey relatively easy.

ACKNOWLEDGMENTS

Writing a book takes time and lots of efforts – plus about the agony in researching and compiling your materials and maximizing the resources available.

This book would not have been possible without the support and encouragement of my family who's always behind my back cheering and supporting all my endeavors.

There are also people and colleagues in the same profession who supported and encouraged me during this process – to where they are pushing me to finish this long delayed guidebook. I say thank you for all your encouragement and support.

To the publisher and the whole staff – from editors, illustrators, graphic designers; thank you for making this dream a reality.

And most of all – I acknowledged the source of knowledge and infinite wisdom, to GOD be the Glory.

INTRODUCTION

Safety begins, and ends, with people.

For the safety professionals, it should not just be about the job title nor the money. For the employers, it should not just be all about saving money nor it's not just all about compliance.

It's all about people – because people make up the business and if you don't have good and safety conscious people, or if people are getting hurt or injured all the time, you don't stay in business very long.

Health and safety is universal - regardless of where people live, people have a vested interest in safety and in their own well-being.

To the safety professionals and those aspiring to be one – we must remember that our motivation for taking and passing NEBOSH is more than our desire for career advancement. It should be that we learn from the course and apply the knowledge that we gained, as applicable, so we can make our workplace safe so there will be no unnecessary harm to people.

The way to sell health and safety to the top management is to show how superior Health and Safety management and programs delivers a return on investment. You measure the number of hours saved by having productive people at work, and by not having to bring in temporary labor because somebody gets injured. You also need to measure the reduction of medical costs and other indirect costs associated with accidents in your company before and after you implement your program. It's all about asset management.

There are many costs of safety not considered beyond the obvious medical costs and regulatory fines. Add in the productivity lost when a permanent employee is not there and a temporary laborer, possibly prone to injury, takes over. There is also an added cost of overtime that might be required to replace the missing employee.

My former boss once said: "You have a very noble job because it transcends beyond your take home pay – your effective leadership and people management literally is protecting people's lives.

Just as in any endeavor, building and implementing a world-class safety program must set its sights on accomplishments - not measurement of failures.

How? By identifying and eliminating, if not minimizing the hazards and the risks of accidents or the number of injuries, you can improve your operational efficiency. Your people will be more productive and motivated and you can also reduce the costs associated to every accidents. And the fact that you are taking care of your people not to get injured or harmed - that's what's important.

Ultimately we are all leaders in here because we're looking out for each other and committed to the overall goal of having a safer work environment.

The way we should operate our business should be: "NO HARM TO PEOPLE AND NO HARM TO ENVIRONMENT".

If you're reading this book right now – it means that either you are planning to enroll or if not currently enrolled in any NEBOSH course and you are scheduled to sit in the exam after you're done with your course.

Because of the learnings and hardships I and with other aspiring NEBOSH candidates encountered when preparing for the exams – I was inspired to write this and hopefully it can help you as well to pass your next exam.

All the best.

And as I've said, "Don't Study Hard – Just Study SMART."

HOW TO USE THIS BOOK

The intention of this book is to guide students or candidates on how to prepare better for the dreaded NEBOSH exams. I've known several fellow students who, after sitting in the exam, felt that everything is fine – only to receive a failed mark when the results are out. I have personal experience and acquaintances of candidates and colleagues in the safety profession who failed to pass the same exam for 2 to 3 occasions.

The first chapter walks you through the basic NEBOSH terminologies, the different classifications and qualifications. If you are enrolled in any NEBOSH qualifications – then you may skip this part. Or if you want to know other NEBOSH courses, then you can also scan through it.

The latter part attempts to share to you my personal experiences and the techniques I used when I took my NEBOSH IGC and NEBOSH International Diploma exams – all of which I passed on my first take.

I hope that as you read through this book and as you remember the techniques and tips I mentioned here, you will face your NEBOSH exams better prepared and you can expect not just to pass - but a 'credit' or 'distinction' grade.

Read on.

CHAPTER 1

NEBOSH AT A GLANCE

What is NEBOSH?

NEBOSH stands for **National Examination Board Occupational Safety Health**.

The NEBOSH is an awarding body based in UK and was formed in 1979 and is also approved by Scottish Qualifications Authority (SQA) Accreditation.

NEBOSH doesn't deliver health and safety training courses; instead it provides syllabuses, exams and assignments to Accredited Course providers or centers, who in turn deliver training courses to prepare candidates for **NEBOSH** qualifications.

NEBOSH courses offers a comprehensive range of globally recognized qualifications designed to meet the Health, Safety and Environmental management needs of all places of work in basically many industries, and national and local government organizations.

NEBOSH qualifications attract approximately around 50,000 candidates annually and different courses are offered by over 600 accredited course providers, with exams taken in over 120 countries around the world.

What are the different NEBOSH classifications?

There are three basic NEBOSH classifications:

1. **NEBOSH's Award-level qualifications** – these provide a basic understanding of Health and Safety principles and practice and provide a perfect introduction to other NEBOSH qualifications.

NEBOSH's Certificate-level qualifications - The NEBOSH Certificate is UK's most popular health and safety qualification. Because it's so well-known and highly regarded, it's ideal if you're looking to launch a career in safety. And although it's useful to have some prior knowledge on safety, there are no formal entry requirements. It provides a good foundation in health and safety for managers, supervisors and staff with health and safety among their day to day responsibilities.

The course itself is divided into three units, the first two are assessed by exams and the third one by a practical assessment. Once completed, the successful candidates meet the academic requirements for Technical Membership of IOSH (Tech IOSH) and associate membership of the IIRSM.

For those working overseas, there is also an increasingly popular demand for NEBOSH International Certificate qualifications.

2. **NEBOSH's Diplomas** - are globally recognized professional qualifications for health, safety and environmental practitioners.

The **NEBOSH Diploma** is a prestigious and highly respected qualification, ultimately enabling Chartered Member of IOSH (CMIOSH) status. Divided into four units (i.e. three assessed by exams and one by an assignment), it's a rigorous and demanding course which nevertheless grows in popularity as safety professionals continue to recognize the benefits of holding such a qualification.

As a quick view, these are the different courses available for certain NEBOSH qualifications.

NEBOSH Certificate Qualifications

1. Health and Safety at Work Qualification

2. National General Certificate in Occupational Health and Safety

3. National Certificate in Construction Health and Safety

4. National Certificate in Fire Safety and Risk Management

5. National Certificate in the Management of Health and Well-being at Work

6. Certificate in Environmental Management

7. International General Certificate in Occupational Health and Safety

8. International Certificate in Construction Health and Safety

9. International Certificate in Fire Safety and Risk Management

10. International Technical Certificate in Oil and Gas Operational Safety

11. NEBOSH Award in Environmental Awareness at Work

12. NEBOSH Award in Health and Safety Environment in the Process industry

NEBOSH Diploma Qualifications

1. Environmental Diploma

2. National Diploma in Occupational Health and Safety

3. International Diploma in Occupational Health and Safety

What is the difference between a NEBOSH Certificate and Diploma?

Actually both are internationally accepted safety qualifications but the NEBOSH National or International General Certificate is a sort of an introduction to the basics of Occupational Health and Safety and covers the management of Health and Safety and a wide variety of hazards in the workplace. Normally, this is ideal for anyone who wants to establish a career in Health and Safety.

The Diploma course is highly recommended for those who have already achieved the NEBOSH International General Certificate or equivalent.

How is a NEBOSH Examination structured?

For NEBOSH IGC, there are 3 Examinations namely:

- IGC 1 - Management of international health and safety
- IGC 2 - Control of workplace hazards
- IGC 3 - Health and safety practical application

For NEBOSH Diploma on Occupational Health and Safety, there are three (3) Examinations namely:

Unit A - composed of ten (10) chapters

A1 - *Principles of health and safety management*
A2 - *Loss causation and incident investigation*
A3 - *Measuring and reviewing health and safety performance*
A4 - *Identifying hazards, assessing and evaluating risk*
A5 - *Risk control*
A6 - *Organizational factors*
A7 - *Human factors*
A8 - *Principles of health and safety law*
A9 - *Criminal law*
A10 - *Civil law*

Unit B – composed of eleven (11) chapters

B1 - *Principles of toxicology and epidemiology*

B2 - *Hazardous substances and other chemicals - assessment of risk*

B3 - *Hazardous substances and other chemicals engineering controls and personal protective equipment*

B4 - *Monitoring and measuring*

B5 - *Biological agents*

B6 - *Physical agents noise and vibration*

B7 - *Physical agents radiation*

B8 - *Psychosocial agents*

B9 - *Musculoskeletal risks and controls*

B10 - *Work environment risks and controls*

B11 - *Managing occupational health*

Unit C – composed of eleven (11) chapters

C1 - General workplace issues

C2 - Principles of fire and explosion

C3 - Workplace fire risk assessment

C4 - Storage, handling and processing of dangerous substances

C5 - Work equipment (general)

C6 - Work equipment (workplace machinery)

C7 - Work equipment (mobile, lifting and access)

C8 - Electrical safety and Electricity at Work Regulations 1989

C9 - Construction hazards and controls

C10 - Workplace transport and driving for work

C11 - Pressure system hazards and controls

Unit D – a detailed review of the health and safety of a workplace or organization, producing a plan to improve performance and applying your knowledge gained from Units A, B and C.

You must pass all exams to be NEBOSH certified. However if you fail in any unit, you can simply re-sit for the one you failed.

Also, after passing the exam and for each paper, the candidate will receive the corresponding certificates. If the candidate pass all 3 papers- they are given 4 certificates: IGC 1, IGC 2, IGC 3 and NEBOSH IGC

Certificates and 5 certificates for the NEBOSH Diploma.

How is the NEBOSH Training structured?

When or before selecting a course provider or the NEBOSH accredited center, you should consider which course and mode of study is suitable for your needs and time availability. NEBOSH courses are carried out in any of the following:

1. **Full Time Training course** – requires you to come to the course provider training center for certain number of days or weeks or even months for classroom type of learning.

2. **Online Learning** – as the name suggests, this type of training offers the courses where students must access the course online depending on his own schedule. Often, an online course tutor is available. This is self-learning and requires

discipline from the student to finish his course on time.

3. **Blended Learning** – this can be a hybrid between full time training and self-study. Some course providers will have classroom sessions, mock examinations, revisions and assignments.

What is the minimum Educational requirement, age or work experience to take the NEBOSH?

There is no clear guideline on the minimum requirements but it would be beneficial if you had relevant working experience in the field of health and safety to be able to relate to the terms used in the course.

As long as the candidate can read and write English, he/she is eligible to take the NEBOSH examinations. Anyway, the course provider or training center will inform you so if there will be changes of this rule.

How long will it take?

This will depend on which type or structure of the course (e.g. online, full time, blended), course provider and what qualification you study. As a rough guide, **Certificate courses** can take from two weeks to a couple of months. **Diploma courses** can take between nine and thirty six months to complete depending on the course providers timetable and the pace at which you wish to proceed in your studies. Normally Diploma courses have a validity period of 5 years.

Here's a sample time schedule for NEBOSH Diploma course:

Unit IA	79 hours tuition and 75 hours private study	Total: 154 hours
Unit IB	71 hours tuition and 50 hours private study	Total: 121 hours
Unit IC	75 hours tuition and 50 hours private study	Total: 125 hours
Unit ID	6 hours tuition and 50 hours private study	Total: 56 hours

A programme of study therefore needs to be based around a minimum of 231 taught hours and approximately 225 hours of private study for an overall total of 456 Hours.

A full-time block release course would be expected to last for a minimum of six weeks (thirty-five working days) and a part-time day release course would be spread over at least thirty weeks. For candidates studying by open or distance learning, the tuition hours should be added to the recommended private study hours to give the minimum number of hours that this mode of study will require.

Tuition time should normally be allocated proportionate to the tuition time for each element but may require adjustment to reflect the needs of a particular student group.

What are the common exam dates for NEBOSH?

1. **For NEBOSH General Certificates** - standard examination sittings are held four times a year in **March, June, September** and **December.**

   Many course providers may also offer on demand examinations, set and marked by NEBOSH but held on a date chosen by the course provider. For this arrangements, you should contact your chosen course provider for more information.

2. **For NEBOSH Diploma** - Examinations will normally be held each year in the third full week of January and in the first full week of July unless prior notice has been given beforehand. Papers for Units A, B and C shall be offered on the mornings of Tuesday, Wednesday and Thursday respectively.

Students eligible to register for any examination and assignment are those enrolled with NEBOSH, with a valid (not expired) enrolment period before the actual exam or before the deadline of the assignment submission date.

CHAPTER 2

GETTING STARTED

NEBOSH command words

Understanding the command words and how to deal with it is perhaps the most important yet often neglected point committed by the students. This is the first and probably the most important point that students must **learn and understand by heart.**

I tell you, based on my experience and from the feedback of my colleagues who failed during the exam – one possible reason on why they failed is not mainly because of lack of knowledge or experience; but more so because of failing to appropriately use and apply the command words in constructing their answers.

These definitions below are used for common understanding of the command words used in the NEBOSH question papers.

Command Words for Certificate Qualifications

Version 1 March 2013

Command Word	Definition
Identify	To give reference to an item, which could be its name or title. *N.B. normally a word or phrase will be enough, provided the reference is clear.*
Give	To offer for consideration, acceptance, or use of another.
	N.B. Give an example of; Give the meaning of

Outline	To indicate the principal features or different parts of. *N.B. an exhaustive description is not required. What is sought is a brief summary of the major aspects of whatever is stated in the question*
Describe	To give a detailed written account of the distinctive features of a subject. The account should be factual, with no attempt to explain. N.B. *When describing a subject (or object) a test of enough detail would be that another person could visualize what you are describing.*

Explain	To provide an understanding. To make an idea or relationship clear. N.B. *this command word is testing the candidate's ability to know or understand why or how something happens. Is often associated with the words 'how' or 'why'.*

1. **List** external sources of health and safety information

   Answer:

   - Health and Safety Executive (HSE) Guidance
   - HASAWA Act
   - Approved Codes of Practice
   - Statutes and legal standards
   - insurance company providers
   - local or business regulations

2. **Give** examples of how employees may misunderstand a verbal instruction

Answer:

- Misinterpreting the message due to lack of understanding of vocabulary;
- Misunderstanding the message due to a language barrier;
- Not hearing the message because of background noise;
- Not hearing the message due to distractions as a result of a busy work area

3. **Outline** the key elements of a permit-to-work system.

Answer:

- The key elements of a permit to work (PTW) system would include the relevant documentation on which the permit activities, hazards and subsequent precautions are recorded.

- The system which supports the PTW would include the need for issue, receipt and return. Additionally there should be a system in place for transferring permits between shifts where appropriate to ensure that activities are not missed or precautions unnecessarily removed.
- There should also be systems in place for the cancellation of the permits where the permit issuer should:
- Check that the work is complete
- Ensure that operations may be returned to normal service, e.g. All isolations have been removed and the equipment is safe to operate and
- Sign the permit off

Command Words for Diploma Qualifications

Version 1 July 2014

Command Word	Definition
Analyze	To divide or break down the subject matter or topic into parts, reasons, aspects, etc. and then examine their nature and relationship
Assess	To present judgments of the factors raised, their significance, importance and why they are important and/or significant.
Calculate	To ascertain or determine by mathematical processes
Comment	To give opinions (with justification) on an issue or statement by considering the issues relevant to it.
Compare & contrast	To provide a point by point account of the similarities and differences between two sets of information or two areas.

Consider	To offer some detail about an issue or event and to deliberate about the value of that issue/event.
Define	To give the meaning of a word, phrase or concept, determine or fix the boundaries or extent of. A relatively short answer, usually one or two sentences, where there is a generally recognized or accepted expression.
Demonstrate	To prove or clarify by reasoning or evidence how some relationship or event has occurred
Describe	To give a detailed written account of the distinctive features of a subject. The account should be factual, with no attempt to explain.
Determine	To come to a decision as the result of investigation or reasoning.
Discuss	To give a critical account of the points involved in the topic.

Distinguish	To present the differences between; to separate into kinds, classes, or categories.
Evaluate	To determine the value or character of something by careful appraisal.
Explain	To provide an understanding. To make an idea or relationship clear.
Give	To offer for consideration, acceptance, or use of another.
Identify	To give reference to an item, which could be its name or title.
Justify	To prove or show to be valid, sound, or conforming to fact or reason.
Outline	To indicate the principal features or different parts of.
Recommend	To bring forward as being fit or worthy; to indicate as being one's choice for something.
Review	To make a survey of; examine, look over carefully and give a critical account.

Responding to the command words appropriately

Using command words appropriately could be the missing link between pass and fail. It is so important to read the whole question and to understand what the question requires as a whole, before attempting to write your answer.

Many candidates miss out in **gaining full marks** because they do not read the question carefully enough and do not think about their answer thoroughly before writing it down.

Some candidates are confident that they are knowledgeable about the question and wrote their answers according to their understanding and not based on what is asked in the question.

In my case, during the exam I always – and I mean **ALWAYS**, ask these questions in my mind.

1. What is/are the command word/s?

2. What do I must say or write to gain full marks?
3. What is and what is not relevant to the question?

Understanding (not just knowing) the command words in a question is the key to success in answering it. The usually **boldly-written** command word indicates the nature of your answer and the skills being assessed.

Question: **Identify** four types of safety sign and **give** an example in EACH case. (8)

Enough answers would include:

1. Prohibition signs – e.g. No smoking
2. Warning signs – e.g. Caution hot surface
3. Mandatory signs – e.g. Wear eye protection
4. Emergency or safe condition signs – e.g. fire exit

Analysis:

1. How many points are given for this question? Ans. 8 points
2. What are the command words?

Ans. IDENTIFY and GIVE - this means you need to identify at least four (4) signs but you should also give an example for each to gain full marks.

Even if you mentioned more than 4 types of safety signs (assuming that there are more than 4) but you failed to give example for each, then you cannot get the full marks but only half of it.

This explains why you should carefully analyze and understand the question.

CHAPTER 3

WHY DO CANDIDATES FAIL IN NEBOSH EXAMINATIONS?

I have a personal experience on this when my colleagues failed during the first sitting. The fact that: we studied together using the same materials; worked on the same company and we are experienced Safety Professionals. At first, I cannot believe why I passed with Distinction while the other four have failed.

So I asked and discussed with them to know the reasons for failure in the NEBOSH examinations.

As expected, their answers were varied such as:

- The questions are tough and misleading

- I was not in good condition during the examination
- I'm working so I could not focus and concentrate on my studies
- My English is poor
- I have answered well but maybe the examiner didn't like my answer
- There wasn't enough time to answer the required questions, etc.

Different answers as expected - but what's really the reasons behind failure in NEBOSH Examinations?

I have analyzed the reasons from my colleagues and from others who failed - and found out the barriers which might be the reasons why they failed to pass or achieve the NEBOSH Certificate on the first sitting.

What are they?

Simply, the reasons are!!

1. Lack of preparation
2. Lack of commitment and focus to study the materials given,
3. Lack of proper guidance on how to study smart (not hard), and
4. Lack of exam techniques.

Admittedly, each and every person are having the plus and minus in terms of comprehension and/or memory. Someone can understand the concepts in a day, some takes a week, some need an hour of guidance or even months.

What's the solution? Is it possible for everyone to pass the NEBOSH examination? The answer is yes! So long as you understand what the examiners are expecting from the candidates.

Remember that NEBOSH examines the level of understanding and they really expect the candidates (safety professionals) to attain a systematic approach and the detailed knowledge about the different safety concepts.

So let's get started.

CHAPTER 4

STUDY AND PREPARATION

Because you have spent time and money for your NEBOSH course - you've committed to take the exam. Then you must prepare way ahead of the exam dates. Here are some tips that I used and which you may find useful:

> **TIP No. 1**
> **Preparation is Key**

1. **Establish your study time** – do it regularly and don't study to the very last minute or within few days before the exam – you'll end up cramming and it will not help you;

2. **Build-up your knowledge** – read and familiarize yourself with the course materials, the technical terms used, case studies, etc. even to the point of reading cross references especially the laws and regulations mentioned;

3. **Practice your reading skills** – try to read and understand, not to memorize the whole context. You will be overwhelmed just by the sheer volume of study materials to read;

4. **Develop your handwriting skills** – make sure that your handwriting is legible and readable because people (not machines) are checking your exam papers; if they can't read your answers, they can't give you marks;

5. **Practice answering** – whether it is from the course material (e.g. end of chapter questions) or from previous exams, you must practice writing your answers;

TIP No. 2
Make some notes when you study

Due to the sheer volume of the reading materials which contains hundreds and even thousands of pages - it helps when you do some "active" studying rather than just reading.

When I study, I'm making my own notes as well. I do not rewrite the whole course but just bullet points on important terms and I try and make it short and easy to read.

I usually based my notes on the learning objectives we are expected to learn from each study unit.

TIP No. 3
Study and be familiar with the Examiners Reports

Normally, NEBOSH will produce and publish examiners reports for most exams. These reports summarizes the exam questions, give the expected or ideal answers and point out where many candidates didn't do well in a particular question.

Personally, this tip works well for me – because even if I don't have to read thoroughly and remember all the course materials, these examiners report give me an overview of how a question must be answered in order to gain full marks.

TIP No. 4
Practice answering previous NEBOSH Exam Papers

You can obtain past question papers and Examiners' Reports from the NEBOSH website (www.nebosh.org).

You should aim to practice answering questions and then check your answer against the Examiners' comments.

There are often repeated questions on exams, so having practiced a good selection may help with repeated questions during your actual exam.

But then again, be careful of the command words used and what is asked in the question. At first, the question may looked similar - but when you read it carefully, they may not be exactly the same, because the key words, the situation and what is required may not be the same.

If you study and analyzed all the previous questions and prepare a good answer; you will have a strong chance to pass the exam.

TIP No. 5
Do the mock exam

The best way of preparing for what you must face on exam day is by practicing exam questions. From the course materials or previous exams, let yourself or somebody prepare random questions from each unit - to be answered within the allocated time, depending on which course you are taking - whether it's for Certificate or Diploma courses.

A word of warning – don't let exam day be the first time you attempt an exam question!

TIP No. 6
Check your answers against the ideal

If possible, let someone help you to check your answer, and note unanswered questions.

For me, I compare my answers with the NEBOSH examiners reports to gauge if I understood the question correctly and if I answered it the way it is being asked.

TIP No. 7
Study one module at a time

When I did my NEBOSH Diploma, I opted to do the exam one at a time so that I could put all my efforts just into one module. I then spent time going over past papers and, more importantly, examiners reports and looking at the comments and 'model answers' and constantly going over it so that I become familiar with the subject.

TIP No. 8
Don't hesitate to ask when in doubt

Asking questions when in doubt is a powerful tool. So do not hesitate to ask your doubts to the trainers, or your tutor who are more than willing to support you so you will excel during examinations.

Better clear your doubts before you appear in examinations, if you do that, then there is no opportunity to doubt your results.

TIP No. 9
Attend Revision or Coaching Session

Attend the revision courses which are offered by the safety professionals team or a certain organization to keep yourself up to date and obviously clear your doubts too.

Don't miss the exam time tips from the safety experts which will have a significant role during examinations.

CHAPTER 5

COMMON PITFALLS

By default, students invest their time to prepare for their scheduled exams. Unfortunately, majority of the examinees, especially for NEBOSH Diploma course, fail on their first or even second attempt.

When the results are out, I tried to talk to my colleagues and batch mates positively hoping that they too passed the recent exam considering that we studied the same materials, we invested (more or less) the same time to study and they too are experienced health and safety professionals.

So, just like them, I also asked – why ! or what happened? Then based on their testimonies and some feedbacks in different forums, I figured out some of the most common pitfalls that the students commit during the exam.

This list may not be comprehensive but at least it should give you an idea on how to avoid these common pitfalls.

1. Candidates did not read the question carefully or did not understand the question properly

It seems to be a particular shortcoming - that candidates do not read the question properly. They provide answers to the question they might like to be answered, or had anticipated, rather than answering the questions as set.

Sometimes, based on your recall; a question appears to be familiar or similar from previous papers thus you will be tempted to rush in writing your answers based on what you want the question to be rather than what that it is actually being asked. There are sometimes well crafted and comprehensive answers - but are not relevant to the question therefore, you won't gain full marks.

Candidates should note that where there is emphasis in a question (e.g. *by the use of italics*), it is to guide candidates towards a particular point. Reading the question encompasses taking due note of this emphasis.

Solution/s:

1.1 Read and understand the question carefully before you attempt to write your answers. Pay attention to the action verbs in bold letters and answer appropriately.

1.2 Ensure that you understand exactly what is expected from these command words or instructions and follow them.

1.3 Don't waste time putting loads of information on each point if the question asks you to 'Identify or Name'.

2. Command words are ignored or not appropriately answered

Many candidates fail to apply the command words (also known as action verbs, e.g. describe, outline, etc.). Command words are the instructions that guide the candidate on the depth of the answer required. If, for instance, a question asks the candidate to 'describe' something, then few marks will be awarded to an answer that is an 'outline'. Similarly the command word 'identify' requires more information that a 'list'.

3. Students did not attempt all required questions

- In some instances, candidates do not attempt all the required questions or are failing to provide complete answers. Candidates are advised to always attempt an answer to a compulsory question, even when the mind goes blank. Applying basic health and safety management principles can generate credit worthy points.

Some candidates fail to answer the question set and instead provide information that may be relevant to the topic but is irrelevant to the question and cannot therefore be awarded marks.

4. Time management of questions

Candidates must plan their time effectively. Some candidates fail to make good use of their time and give excessive detail in some answers leaving insufficient time to address all of the questions.

Other candidates unnecessarily wrote the question on their paper which is again a waste of time. It is neither necessary nor desirable for candidates to spend time repeating the question before they commence their answers.

5. Unstructured Answers

Some candidates fail to separate their answers into the different sub-sections of the questions. These candidates could gain marks for the different sections if they clearly indicated which part of the question they were answering (i.e. *by using the numbering from the question in their answer*). Structuring your answers to address the different parts of the question can also help in logically drawing out the points to be made in response.

It is important for candidates to structure their answers as this helps cover all the requirements of the question without losing focus. It is good examination technique to look for the principles or the concepts that underpin the topic and to use those as a basis for delivering a structured answer.

6. Illegible Handwriting

While this is not an examination in handwriting, Examiners should be able to read your answers. In this electronic age, professional people may not need to write text in longhand. However, to pass this examination it is an essential and necessary part of the preparation to rehearse writing questions in full and in the time allocated.

Candidates should also know that examiners cannot award marks if handwriting is illegible.

CHAPTER 6

OVERCOMING PITFALLS

If you are unsure of a question after spending a reasonable amount of time thinking about it, leave enough space as applicable and move on to the next one you can answer. You can come back to the question you are struggling on later. Don't panic, everyone has moments of complete blankness!

Ensure you attempt to answer EVERY question.

Plan your study time! NEBOSH advise you spend at least 51 hours of home study in addition to any classroom hours. Be honest with yourself – are you going to fit in this amount of home study based on your study plan?

Dedicate your time in the exam appropriately. There is no point spending the majority of your time on a question that will gain you minimum marks and then not having enough time to complete the questions with the most allocated marks. You should allocate 9 minutes to a small question ie Q 2-11 and 30 minutes to a more detailed question ie Q1.

When you have put in a good amount of home study then practice your exam technique with past papers, practice your timing to ensure you can complete the paper within the allocated time.

Practice handwriting consistently for 2 hours. Generally we are used to using computers etc. and typing for most of our day and are out of the habit of handwriting! I myself experienced pain on my hand during the actual exam because I'm not used to write straight for 3 hours or so.

Ensure you arrive in good time for the exam. At least 30 minutes before the start time as a minimum.

Read all the instructions on your Admission slip.

Our brains take in information in a number of different ways. If you repeatedly read your revision guides you will find your brain skips information it thinks it knows. Force your brain to take information by studying using different techniques such as:

1. Make yourself a set of key point **quick revision cards**. Carry a set with you to study over a coffee shop, get your colleagues to quiz you. Might sound silly but stick them around your house for a quick reminder. You'll be surprised at how well this works! This technique works well for bullet point informations, mnemonics etc.

2. **Mind Mapping** - An easy visual way of learning

    ♣ Write out your notes
    ♣ Create a visual 'picture' to imagine the answer

3. Record your key information points onto your mp3 or cd etc. to enable you to listen to these whilst in the car, out for run etc.

4. The best way to ensure information sticks is ***Repetition, Repetition, Repetition!***

How much and how long should you study?

Straightforward answer is – **"It's up to you…"**

If you're doing a block course (meaning you sit in a class), then either you can do advance reading or you must review the day's lessons in the evening. In this way, the lessons covered during the day will sink in and you won't leave yourself with a mountain to climb just before the exam (often a good way to fail).

If you're doing distance learning, you may find yourself with several weeks of revision time, in which case a revision timetable will always be a good idea – look at the time you have left, then divide it up so you spend roughly equal time on each element.

Diploma revision will take at least six weeks per unit – preferably ten. A revision period of up to ten weeks will enable you to focus on one element per week.

How you revise is up to you. Some people read the notes carefully, making their own summary notes followed by testing themselves by doing past exam questions. Others make up packs of revision cards with key points they read through on the bus or train, or when they have a few spare minutes – ultimately, it's up to you to decide on the method that suits you best.

Don't neglect your revision – this is where the real learning takes place. Making plans at an early stage and having a clear strategy for what exams to take and when to take them will pay dividends.

CHAPTER 7
EXAM TECHNIQUES

Exam Success

I just read in some publications but I did not verify if this empirical formula is backed up by research and statistics – but just the same, based on my experience I agree with what is written below:

1. **Innate ability (20%)** – this could mean your IQ or stored knowledge, your analytical skills, including your comprehension skills and most importantly – your handwriting skills

2. **Good knowledge of the subject (30%)** – as mentioned, being familiar and having read the

course syllabus or having a direct and relevant experience in the workplace – you can still earn points.

3. **Strong exam technique (50%)** – this is often overlooked by the students. Like what I mentioned in Chapter 3 and by appropriately using the command words – you will for sure get higher if not full marks on each question.

Applying the Command Words

Again, remember that all NEBOSH questions have an "action verb" or "command words" which would provide you a tip on how much detail should be included in your answer.

For Example:

1. Questions starting with **"Outline"**, **"Identify"** or **"List"** indicate that little depth in your answer is required. Simple as it may, but again there's a difference between the instructions.

For these types of questions simply mentioning the key features and the types are necessary. No need to explain them.

However, if you provide a simple 'list' when an 'outline' was asked for, or vice versa - you will NOT be able to get full marks or maximum points – plain and simple.

For the 'outline' type of questions, one of the common mistakes is that the candidate starts to explain the answer. In these type of questions you don't need to explain the key features, simply mentioning is enough.

2. Questions with "**Describe**" or "**Explain**" as command words require much greater depth – a paragraph type of answer is ideal because bullet-point answers will probably not be detailed enough to gain full marks.

Sometimes, you might come across with exam questions that will give you a specific instruction e.g. draft a management report or draft a proposal to management, etc.

Here, you must show or explain and/or justify your answers and arguments as if you are a safety professional trying to convince or seek approval from top management - who might be unfamiliar with health & safety.

In NEBOSH Diploma or even in NEBOSH Certificate exams, there are longer questions which has 20 marks or points.

In this case, it is VERY important that before you start to answer, you must come up (even mentally) some sort of a plan. It could be a mind map, a diagram or a table – which will guide you how to structure or present your answers. This way, you can make sure you cover all the points and items being asked and put it in your answer.

Time Management

Depending on which NEBOSH exam you are taking, there is always a time limit. Note that there is also additional 10 minutes reading time before the start of the exam.

In the NEBOSH IGC, time allowed is 2 hours and there are eleven (11) questions on each paper and you are expected to answer them all. See below ideal allocation of each question.

	Points	Time allocation	Total time
Question 1	20 each	25 minutes	25 mins
Questions 2-11	8 each	8 minutes	80 mins
		Total time	105 mins.
		Spare time	15 mins

So, if you strictly follow the allocated time for each question, you still have a small spare time (15 minutes) at the end to check over your paper, review your answers or attempt those questions that are left out.

In the NEBOSH International Diploma, 3 hours is allocated plus 10 minutes additional reading time before the examination. Note that you are not allowed to write anything during this period. Use this 10 minutes to scan the questions to get a 'feel' of it and somehow decide which one to answer first. The question you are familiar with or the one you are confident to answer first.

Section A contains six (6) questions which carries equal marks (normally 10 points each) and you are required to answer them all. It is advised that you need to spend about **15 minutes** on each question.

For Section B, there are 5 questions which carries 20 points each – but you only need to select and answer 3 of them. You should need to spend about 30 minutes on each question. This is how it looks like:

	Points	Time allocation	Total time (180 mins)
Section A Questions 1 – 6	10 each	10 mins. each	60 mins
Section B Questions 1 – 3	20 each	30 mins. each	90 mins
		Total time	150 mins.
		Spare time	30 mins

Having said this, you must be disciplined and observe strict time management.

So, you must plan your answer. If a question is split into parts, note the points or marks allocated and spend a proportionate amount of time on each part without spending too much time on a single part of a question and leave the other parts unanswered.

It's all too easy to get comfortable answering a question you know well only to find that you've made

50 good points on a 20 mark question - and so it's as if you wasted 30 marks and time. Because of this, you now have barely enough time left to pick up any marks for the others.

And if you run out of time, you can make an attempt by making basic points for remaining questions – rather leave it blank which results to zero mark.

> **Hot Tip!**
> **Before you sit the exam, work out how much time would allow you for each question and STICK TO IT.**

Please remember:

1. It is better to provide an answer to every question than to do 9 or 10 of them very well. Those 2 or 3 marks you manage to grab here might just make the difference.

2. It's also worth remembering that for any question you failed to attempt, your score will

be ZERO! So, answer every question, even if you're not confident and sure of your answer.

3. If you have reached the time limit as mentioned in the exam timing - MOVE ON!

4. You should not waste time trying to give a perfect answer to a question - if it means you will run out of time to attempt the other remaining questions.

5. Be brief and concise. You will not get extra points for a long, rambling answer especially if it is not relevant to the question.

6. Don't be tempted to keep writing and writing because you know the question or the subject well – there are no additional marks or points for that. For example, if 'list' is the command word – don't give an answer in paragraph form.

Preparing for the Actual Exam

First Things First!

Assuming you have gone through the whole course materials for the past few weeks, or months or even years (for the Diploma), then you prepare yourself physically and mentally for sitting in the exam.

Here are some suggestions on what you can do to prepare yourself for the highly anticipated examination days.

The Day before the exam

- If you are working and if it is possible, you might need to take a day off from your job;
- Check and prepare what to bring (e.g. pens, extra pens, calculators, valid ID's, exam voucher, etc.);
- Check the time and venue for your exam – so you can estimate your travelling time. Better if

you can go the venue and know your assigned room number;

- Have a good night's sleep. Don't go out the night before the exam or stay up until late;
- If possible, do not anymore read your study materials – the more you do, the more your brain will be stressed out;
- Eat a balanced meal. Avoid fatty foods, alcohol and/or junk foods

On The Day (before the exam)

- Eat breakfast – your brain and your body needs fuel and energy;
- Have a wrist watch and double check the exam requirements (exam voucher, pens, ID's, etc.);
- Arrive at the examination center ahead of time (30 minutes minimum) especially if you have not visited it the day before;
- Locate your assigned exam room and/or the invigilator;

- Again, AVOID last minute reading of your notes or course materials – it will only make you freak out;
- As much as possible, avoid discussions with other students about the subject;
- Breathe and relax – and wait for the time.

During the exam

- Listen first to the general instructions made by the invigilator or testing officer;
- Strictly follow the exam instructions;
- Maximize the reading time. You are given approximately 5 minutes to read through the questions in General Certificates and 10 minutes allocated for Diploma;
- Clearly mark each page and each part of your answer with the question number;
- Always start on a new page for every question even if you still have enough space left within the page from the previous questions;

- Watch out for the time but you can take mini-breaks – you may go to the washroom or have something ready to eat;
- Use only generally accepted NEBOSH acronyms i.e. MSD's, RIDDOR, etc.
- If you are sick or if you feel unwell tell the invigilator or testing officer;
- Also you must ensure that you understand what you've have read. If you are having problems, you can clarify them to your invigilator or testing officer;
- Do not put unnecessary marks in any part of the questionnaire;
- Even if you're done with all the questions and have reviewed your answers – you may still stay until the end.

Just before you write your answers

To emphasize how important this technique – I shall say this again.

Start by reading the exam paper and the questions all the way through.

There might be an awkward, obscure question on the exam paper. **Don't panic.**

My advice is to start first on an easy question to get the confidence going (this is my preference) as you can answer the questions in any order you choose.

You should find at least one question you are familiar with or confident about answering. The pages in your answer book are numbered according to the question you are answering, so it doesn't matter in which order you answer the questions, as long as you put your answer on the corresponding page of the answer book. It's a good idea to start with the question you're most familiar with, as this gets your brain working and gives you confidence.

Work through two 'easier' questions first and then work towards the harder ones. Just make sure you attempt them all and ALWAYS follow the time allocated for each question.

Beware though. If you do this, make sure you tick off the questions you have done. It's very easy to reach the end and realize you have missed a question out.

If you are taking the NEBOSH diploma, my advice is to choose very carefully which of the three from five optional 20 point questions to take first. Get these out of the way and put plenty of energy into creating good wholesome answers. It can create the feeling of confidence that you have probably passed the exam before you have even attempt the shorter, compulsory 10 point questions.

Hot Tip!
READ & RE-READ THE QUESTION

Get an idea of what the question is asking. Every word written is there for a reason.

> **Command words are written in bold.**

Re-read the question until you are certain that you exactly understand what is being asked.

This is especially important on questions with some sub-topics and where you answer in part. It is very tempting and easy to rush in to the answer, only to find when you get to the next part (i.e. item xx) that you'll be writing the same thing.

NEBOSH do not ask you to give the same information twice in one question.

So if this is happening, **you're going wrong** and you'll expect no additional marks there.

So READ IT again (and again), before you start writing!

Do not answer just because you feel you knew the subject. Instead, answer what is specific to the question.

You can do some quick mental exercise and ask yourself:

- *What is the command word? (in bold type)*
- *What aspects of the topic are you being asked to consider?*
- *How many parts are there in the question?*
- *How many marks are allocated for this question?*

This will give you an idea of the depth of answer required, denoted by the command words or action verbs (e.g. outline, describe, state, list, etc.). It also focuses your mind on how to structure your answers.

It is a good idea to highlight the important words in the question, either by underlining them or by using a highlighter pen (ask first if this is allowed). Again, this clarifies what you are being asked and allows you to think about what your answer should be.

Answering Question in 'parts'

This happens especially on question having 20 marks i.e. question no. 1 for NEBOSH IGC or any of the 3 questions in Part B of NEBOSH International Diploma. Here's what you can do:

- Check if the questions in different parts are related or distinct from each other;
- Single part questions are often dismissed as complex and difficult but can often be split into distinct parts;
- The marks or points allocated indicate how much weight are given to each part of the answer;
- Determine what is required by each part;
- Don't repeat your answer in part b when the same information was already given in part a
- Clearly separate which is your part 'a', part 'b' or part 'x' answers

Once you've started your answer, check the question to make sure you're answering what you've been asked.

I knew some of my colleagues who rushed on their answers and have gone off tangent to these type of NEBOSH questions. They thought they've given perfect answers on one part – then found out they run out of ideas for the succeeding parts.

Prioritizing and Clustering

This means that you need to plan or map out your answer before writing it down on paper.

For example, if the question asks for hierarchy of controls, you should not rush and ramble on your answers for it will appear cluttered and you will not gain full marks.

In this case, prioritizing means you need to consider the proper hierarchy of considering controls such as:

1. **Elimination** – eliminate or avoid the hazard (if possible)
2. **Substitution** – use something else which for example are less hazardous, etc.
3. **Engineering Controls** – controlling the hazards through design or by guarding or isolation
4. **Administrative controls** – minimize risk through training, safe procedures, etc.
5. **Personal Protective Equipment (PPE)** – use only as last resort

Clustering or grouping your answers are applicable for questions that can be grouped or clustered together.

For example, question about manual handling. You can group your answer in sub topics using an acronym TILE.

> **Task (T)** - think about how often or how much twisting or bending is involved

Individual (I) – it pertains about individual capabilities whether male or female, old or young, new or experienced employees, etc.

Load (L) – how heavy is it? Is it bulky? Is it stable or balanced?

Environment (E) – what about the surrounding environment? Is it hot? Cold? Does it involve working at heights or climbing stairs? Etc.

Another example is a question about identifying the **different costs** of accidents.

Since it's an identify type of question, our immediate approach is to list down answers such as hospital costs, insurance cost, overtime, clean-up, etc. depending on the points available.

Well, there's no problem about that, but better answers are clustered/group into **'direct costs'** and **'indirect costs'** – and answering this way earns you better marks.

Practice the mnemonics technique or make an acronym

Mnemonics is an excellent technique which will ensure the number of key points and obviously it will prevent you from the on time memory loss during the examinations.

Example : To Remember the types of Guards in Machines :

F = **F**ixed guard

I = **I**nterlocked Guard

A = **A**djustable Guard

T = **T**rip switch.

Each and every chapters in NEBOSH, there are a number of mnemonics which are really most important for your exam preparations.

Handling "Tricky" Questions

As mentioned earlier, some types of questions appears in the exam - again and again.

My suggestion? Don't rush to write your answer.

Questions that states - "Outline the factors to consider when........" is an example of a 'tricky' question.

This type of question requires you to think about the situations given and you must take an overview.

Take note.

1. You are not asked how to fix it!
2. You do not have to outline a series of control measures BUT just some factors to consider given the scenario.

> **This is a very common mistake on how students approach this type of question.**

Okay, let's get to it in details.

For example:

If you were asked to **outline** *the factors to consider before forklift trucks (FLT's) are to be introduced to a new warehouse.* How would you answer it?

It is tempting to rush by giving answers such as:

When FLTs are to be introduced into the workplace, it is essential that they do not come into contact with pedestrians. To prevent this, dedicated traffic routes should be introduced, implement speed limits or install speed retarders.

Also, any pedestrians who enter the area in which the FLTs are moving should wear appropriate PPE, such as high-visibility vests. And only authorized and trained drivers are allowed to operate.

In a warehouse, you should make sure that if the ventilation is poor, the FLTs should be battery-powered.

The floors should be free from potholes and steep slopes, as this can cause overturning of the FLT, etc.

Now, (mentally) raise your hand if you thought of answering the above question this way. Or you have answered it that way... just be honest to yourself, anyway nobody sees you.

Now that's the common mistake committed by students.

Although the answer is related to the question i.e. about FLT's operation in the warehouse - but that's not actually what the question asked you for.

Remember;

Do not answer just because you feel you knew the subject. But answer what is specific to the question.

So what is really being asked by the question? Let me tell you what.

1. What is the command word? Ans. **Outline**
   - Is the answer above followed an outline format? Yes

2. What aspects of the topic are you being asked to consider? Ans. You are asked about the "factors to consider **BEFORE**..." – which means not during operations

You see the difference?

So I hope it's clear now that the answers written above (although in outline format) are in fact more of a control measures to reduce the risks from FLTs operating in a new warehouse.

So what should be the proper answer/s to the question?

For me, below are some factors to consider before FLT's are to be introduced to a new warehouse.

- The type of FLT to be introduced and the appropriate fuel supply (diesel, LPG or Electric)
- The need to consider space dimensions or hallway or loading/unloading requirements ;
- The need for separating fork lift trucks (FLT) movements from pedestrians;
- The need for the introduction of speed limits;
- Evaluate whether high visibility clothing would be required;
- The condition of the floors and terrain;
- The loads or products to be carried, etc.

Would you get full marks if you answered it this way?

NO!

Because the way it was written/structured is in bullet form which might be considered as 'list' format instead of the required 'outline'.

So, to possibly get the full marks - you should turn this 'list' into an 'outline' format by adding the reason for each consideration you mention.

This is how it should look like;

> ➢ The condition of the floors and terrain - *the condition of the floors and terrain would be an important factor to be considered as floors finishing or floors containing humps, potholes or steep slopes can cause overturning of fork lift trucks.*

When you answered this way, gaining full marks is not a remote possibility.

And last, if the same question is worth 8 points, then if possible, come up with at least 8 answers in 'outline' format i.e. if you can think of more than 8 'factors'.

Another important thing to watch out!

AVOID "ROTE" LEARNING

Rote learning is a memorization technique based on repetition. The idea is that one can quickly recall the meaning of the material the more one repeats it. This is good and applicable for questions on technical terms and definitions but not quite well for scenario based questions.

It's useless to memorize the points. Safety is not a bundle of books or the number of pages - safety is simply an application of common sense with the technical inputs. So don't memorize! It won't help you in the examination, better get a suggestion from the trainers and understand the concepts.

Remember the 'trick' questions and the ones which are similar but differs in command words? If you just memorize your answer, you may find yourself misreading the question and giving an inappropriate answer.

It is much better if you develop and understand the underlying principles or consider the whole scenario – only then you can apply appropriate answers to the question.

Let's try this example:

Question: Members of the public have been injured when collecting baggage from a baggage conveyor at an airport.

Outline control measures that should be in place to reduce the risk of injury from the mechanical hazards.

> ➤ Based on the examiners' report, they observed that some candidates answered this question as though it was about a coal conveyor, stating that nip guards and safety trip wires should be fitted which is of course not applicable for bag conveyors in the airport.

Others suggested that wearing of PPE's such as gloves and boots with steel toecaps is a must. Common sense would tell us that this is only appropriate for staff working as baggage handlers – and not for passengers.

Likewise it is not realistic to expect passengers to avoid wearing loose-fitting clothes and jewelry.

Some candidates also suggested signage saying 'keep away' and keeping passengers at a distance from the conveyor.

Others thought that physical barriers keeping the public away would be useful not realizing that this defeats the object of the baggage conveyor wherein passengers really must be close to the running conveyors to pick-up their luggage.

The above answers is an indicative of a general failing by some candidates to appreciate the practical requirement of the whole scenario and instead rely on 'rote learning' or plain memorization of past examination questions.

When you have finished!

If you have strictly followed your timing to each question, you should have a few extra minutes to spare to check back and run through your answers.

Yes, I know it's boring, but you may think of something you've missed or see a glaring error. It's easier to pick up some extra marks by filling in gaps in questions which require you to list or identify, so if you've missed anything out, now is the final time to check what you've written and see if you've missed anything obvious.

What if I'm running out of time?

If you find yourself with only minutes to spare at the end of the exam, and you still have a question or questions to answer, **complete it as a list**. This at least gives you the chance to get some marks, rather than leaving it blank and scoring zero. The extra marks you may pick up here could make the difference between referral and pass; pass and credit, or even credit and distinction!

After the examination

For sure, there will mixed feelings even after you get out of the exam center. A surge of elation or depression is natural – let it pass. As the saying goes – there's no use crying over a spilled milk; so don't convince yourself you have failed – you only know your performance when you get your results.

I also avoid discussing my answers with other students – I will only feel bad for questions I did not get.

So – What's Next?

Things will get back to normal. The best thing is to wait for the result. If you are convinced that you have not performed well in the exam, then you might review again or you may need to proceed to another unit in the case of NEBOSH Diploma (as long as you did not take the 3 units in one go).

You can also start working for your Unit D assignment upon consultation with your center's tutor.

CHAPTER 8

ONE NOT-SO-COMMON 'FREEBIE'

Yes! There's one not-so-common freebie that 'smart' students can avail of.

> You can use bilingual dictionaries or bilingual translation dictionaries, subject for approval by NEBOSH, so you will have extra 25% additional time.

Although I haven't tried to avail this during any of my exams - but having 25% extra possible time; this is 45 minutes extra for Diploma qualifications – you can do a lot to finish and/or review the remaining questions.

This privilege is for students or candidates whose primary language is not English. Irish (or Gaelic) or Welsh. It is the responsibility of the accredited course provider to verify eligibility.

Using a dictionary should reflect the candidate's normal way of working and it is the responsibility of the accredited course providers to consider whether extra time would be more appropriate.

The candidate's need of the dictionary does not in itself justify allowing the candidate extra time, unless the candidate has to refer to the dictionary so often that examination time is used for this purpose delaying the answering of questions.

Above all, applications must be made known and approved by NEBOSH.

Enquiries About Results (EARs)

NEBOSH supports the right of students and/or accredited course providers to enquire about a result, to appeal against the outcome of that enquiry and has procedures to ensure that such enquiries and appeals are dealt with in a thorough and equitable manner.

If you believe that your result does not match your reasonable expectations, an Enquiry About Result (EAR) must be made in writing within **one calendar month** of issue of the result to which it relates.

What about the assignments?

I purposely did not include it here because it has different set of guidelines and as such, you will also be guided by the center or by a tutor assigned to you (in the case of NEBOSH Diploma).

Also, you will have all the time to edit and have it checked by your colleague or by an experienced Safety Professional before you do the final submission.

ABOUT THE AUTHOR

The author is a Health, Safety and Environment (HSE) consultant and is also a Distinguished Toastmaster, a trainer, content writer, a mentor and a coach.

Because of schedule constraints, he enrolled online and took both NEBOSH IGC and International Diploma. By applying the techniques shared in this book, he passed the exams on his first attempt and earned a Distinction grade in NEBOSH IGC.

Lightning Source UK Ltd.
Milton Keynes UK
UKHW010558240420
362137UK00002B/550